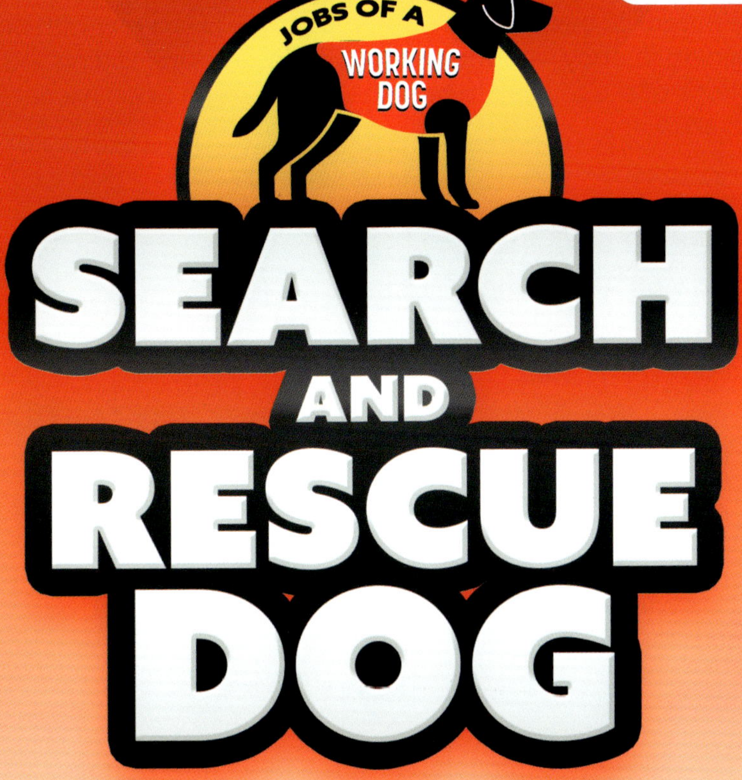

SEARCH AND RESCUE DOG

A Crabtree Branches Book

B. Keith Davidson

CRABTREE
Publishing Company
www.crabtreebooks.com

School-to-Home Support for Caregivers and Teachers

This high-interest book is designed to motivate striving students with engaging topics while building fluency, vocabulary, and an interest in reading. Here are a few questions and activities to help the reader build upon his or her comprehension skills.

Before Reading:

- *What do I think this book is about?*
- *What do I know about this topic?*
- *What do I want to learn about this topic?*
- *Why am I reading this book?*

During Reading:

- *I wonder why...*
- *I'm curious to know...*
- *How is this like something I already know?*
- *What have I learned so far?*

After Reading:

- *What was the author trying to teach me?*
- *What are some details?*
- *How did the photographs and captions help me understand more?*
- *Read the book again and look for the vocabulary words.*
- *What questions do I still have?*

Extension Activities:

- *What was your favorite part of the book? Write a paragraph on it.*
- *Draw a picture of your favorite thing you learned from the book.*

TABLE OF CONTENTS

What Do Search and Rescue Dogs Do?

Search and rescue (SAR) dogs are brought in after a natural or a human-made **disaster**, or when a person has gone missing.

SAR dogs use different methods, such as **tracking** and **air scenting**, to find humans who need help.

Air scenting dogs can find a scent from a quarter mile (0.4 km) away.

When there is a disaster, such as an **avalanche**, mudslide, or earthquake, these dogs are used to find people who are trapped.

This type of searching is called non-scent discriminating. This means they are looking for *any* human, not just one human's scent.

SAR dogs can smell a person buried up to 15 feet (4.6 meters) in snow, mud, or debris from a collapsed building.

Tracking and trailing are different disaster-rescue skills. Dogs used for tracking or trailing are given the scent of one person.

Tracking happens when dogs use their noses to look for certain tracks or markers, such as footsteps or pieces of clothing. Trailing happens when dogs follow the scent wherever it is found, including the air or ground.

A dog that is trailing does not follow a specific set of tracks. It has more independence and follows the scent wherever it leads.

Serving in the Community

Whenever disaster strikes, SAR dogs are brought in to help. Handlers used SAR dogs to help find people after the September 11, 2001 attacks on the World Trade Center in New York City, during Hurricane Katrina in 2005, and when a condominium building collapsed in Florida.

The Champlain Towers collapsed in Surfside, Florida on June 24, 2021.

FACT The job of a SAR handler is not easy. They have to have the skills to take the dogs deep into the wilderness, or into the middle of a natural disaster.

Breeds

The most popular breeds for search and rescue come from the herding, sporting, working, and hound groups.

Border collies are part of the herding group.

Labradors are part of the sporting group.

The bloodhound is probably one of the first breeds people think of when they think of SAR dogs. Known for their incredible sense of smell, they were first used by humans for hunting.

A bloodhound can smell a trail up to 300 hours old—that's 12.5 days!

Herding dogs, such as German and Dutch shepherds, and sporting dogs, such as Labrador and golden retrievers, are known for their loyalty and ability to learn new skills.

These dogs bond with their human partners and are always eager to please them.

The Saint Bernard with a barrel on its collar is a well-known **symbol** of avalanche search and rescue.

The original Saint Bernard dogs did not receive special training. Instead, the older dogs would show the younger dogs how to find people.

FACT

Monks at the hospice of the Great St. Bernard Pass, Switzerland, started using Saint Bernards for avalanche rescues in the 1660s. Saint Bernards are no longer used as rescue dogs today.

Picking the Perfect Puppy

When looking to find a SAR dog, many organizations turn to shelters to find the dogs they need. These rescue dogs are then trained to rescue people in emergencies.

The ideal dog listens well and enjoys hunting for hidden toys.

FACT

SAR dogs need to be capable of working four to eight hours without distraction.

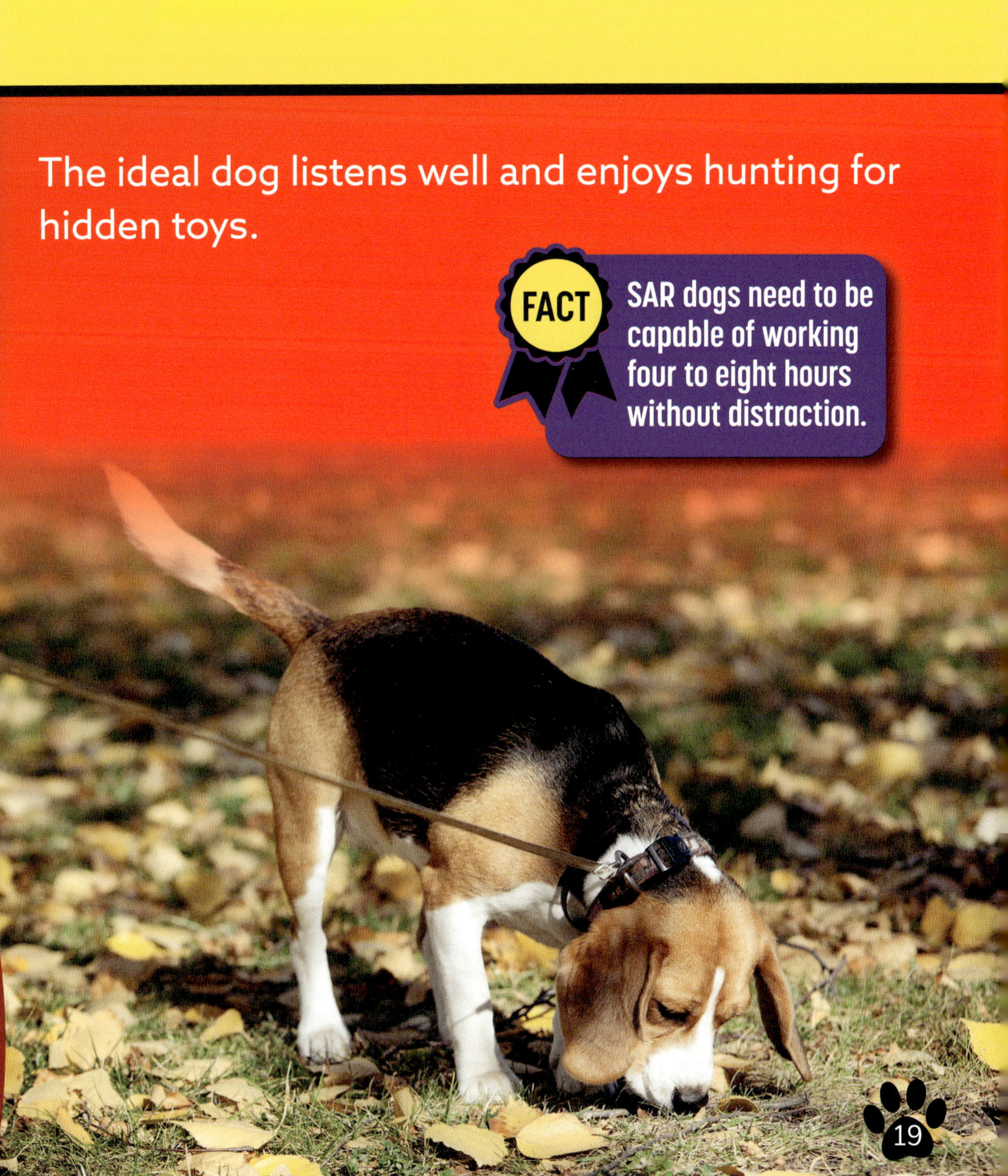

Training

When training a SAR dog, the handler uses rewards and praise for effort and success. For any type of work, the handler has to make sure the dog wants to succeed.

Training often starts with the game of find the ball. A dog that loves to play find the ball for hours will likely make a very good SAR dog.

The basis of SAR training is getting the dog to think a human scent is something it wants to find.

There are different styles of **detection** learning. Tracking involves a dog keeping its nose to the ground and following a trail.

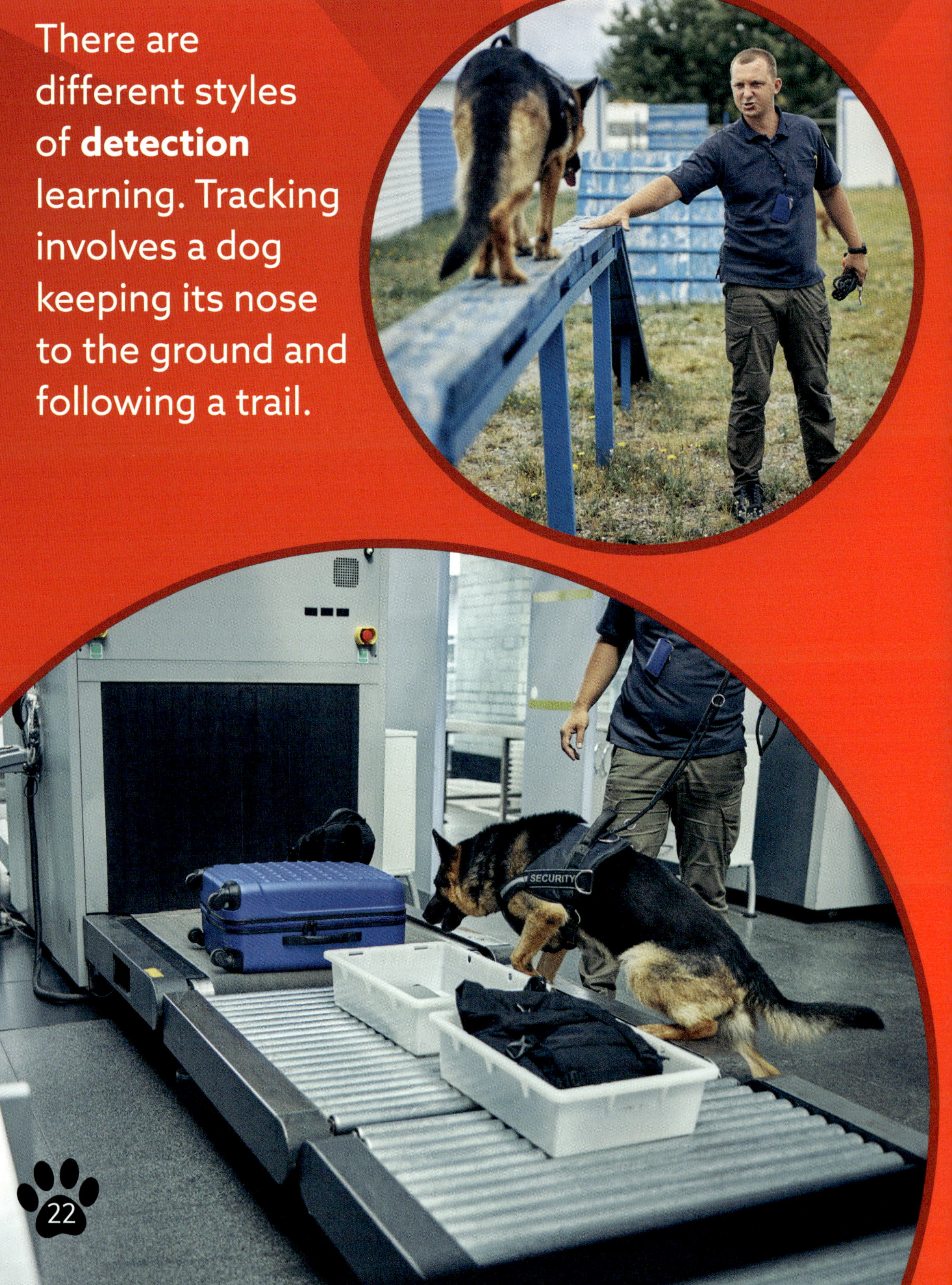

Training a dog for air scenting takes a little longer because the dog must be able to do this off its leash.

The average SAR dog needs 600 hours of training to be ready for work.

SAR dogs also learn different ways to alert their handler when they find people. Some dogs are trained to perform recall-find. This means they find a person in need, return to their handler, and lead the handler to the person. Other dogs are trained to use victim loyalty, in which they stay with the person in need and bark to alert the handler.

SAR dogs can be trained to search the bottom of lakes. They can detect gases that float to the surface.

SAR Dogs Are Heroes!

Jake, the Labrador retriever, is a notable SAR dog. He helped find people buried in the **rubble** of the World Trade Center after it was attacked in 2001.

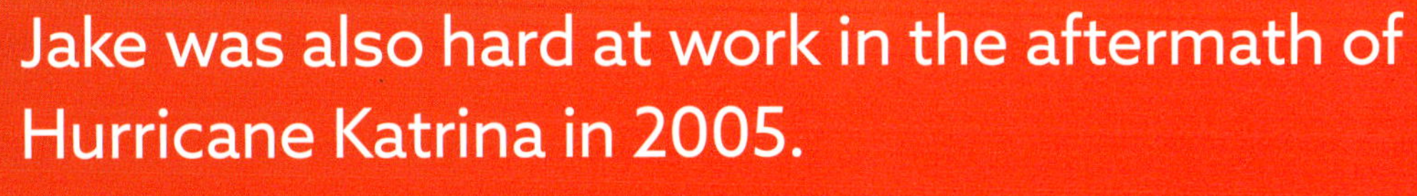

Jake was also hard at work in the aftermath of Hurricane Katrina in 2005.

More than 300 dogs were used to search the rubble in the days following the attacks on the World Trade Center.

Orion, a Rottweiler, helped save the lives of at least 37 people when heavy rains hit coastal mountains in Venezuela in December of 1999. The rain lasted for two days and caused flash flooding and mudslides. Thousands of homes were destroyed.

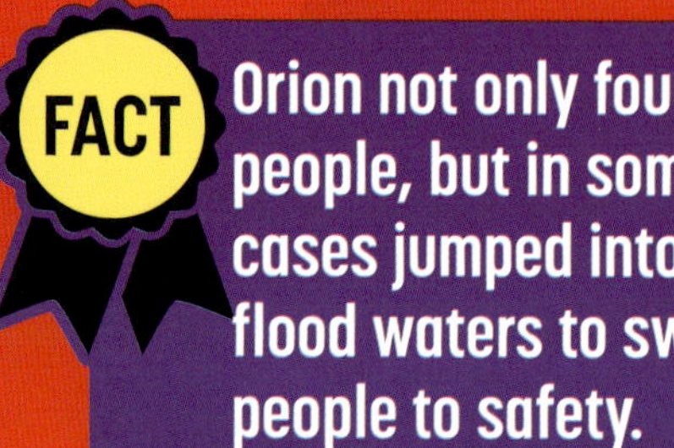

Orion not only found people, but in some cases jumped into the flood waters to swim people to safety.

Rottweilers are big, muscular dogs and are not known to be the best swimmers. Many think this makes Orion an even bigger hero!

Rottweiler

Every day, all over the world, search and rescue dogs are saving lives.

Glossary

air scenting (AIR SENT-ing): detecting a scent in the air and following it off-leash

avalanche (AV-uh-lanch): a large mass of snow, ice, or earth that suddenly moves down the side of a mountain

detection (di-TEK-shun): the act of finding things

disaster (duh-ZASS-tur): an event that causes great damage, loss, or suffering

rubble (RUHB-uhl): broken bricks, stones, or other pieces of a building

symbol (SIM-buhl): a design or object that represents something else

tracking (TRAK-ing): following someone or something

Index

Websites to Visit

http://jcsda.com/kids/sardogs.htm

https://kids.nationalgeographic.com/pages/article/lost-and-found

https://kids.kiddle.co/Dog

About the Author

B. Keith Davidson

B. Keith Davidson grew up around dogs and has always been fascinated by the bonds that humans and these very special creatures share. Beagles are his favorite dogs, even if they are stubborn and frustrating. He has a Master's degree in Canadian History from Carleton University.

Written by: B. Keith Davidson
Designed by: Jennifer Dydyk
Edited by: Kelli Hicks
Proofreader: Janine Deschenes

Photographs: Cover illustration of Dog(also on title page) © Nevada3, photo of dog © Vladimir Staykov, child in the snow © Alonafoto, Page 4 © IV. androme, Page 5 top photo © jasomtomo, bottom photo © hxdbzxy, Page 6 © Noska Photo, Page 7 © David Schliepp, Pages 8 and 9 all photos © Jim Parkin, Page 10 © Noska Photo, Page 11 top photo © Felix Mizioznikov, bottom photo © hxdbzxy, Page 12 collies © xkunclova, Labrador retriever © Dora Zett, Page 13 bottom photo © Edoma, Page 14 © Stoyan Yotov, Page 15 top photo © IV. andromeda, bottom photo © Nikolai Tsvetkov, Page 16 © Ivonne Wierink, Page 17 dogs © KriKo, Hospice © Chaykoi, Page 18 © Christian Mueller, Page 19 © Elena Efimova, Page 20 © bluecrayola, Page 21 © Anaite, Page 22 both photos © YAKOBCHUK VIACHESLAV, page 23 © SasaStock, Page 24 © Noska Photo, Page 25 top photo © Marcella Miriello, bottom photo © Ingrid Pakats, Page 27 © Noska Photo, Page 28 © Giongi63, Page 29 top photo © caseyjadew, bottom photo © Leeloona. All images from Shutterstock.com except for public domain image page 13 (top), page 26 courtesy of FEMA

Library and Archives Canada Cataloguing in Publication

CIP available at Library and Archives Canada

Library of Congress Cataloging-in-Publication Data

CIP available at Library of Congress

Crabtree Publishing Company

www.crabtreebooks.com 1-800-387-7650

 Printed in the U.S.A./CG20210915/012022

 In Canada: We acknowledge the financial support of the Government of Canada through the Canada Book Fund for our publishing activities.

Published in the United States
Crabtree Publishing
347 Fifth Avenue, Suite 1402-145
New York, NY, 10016

Published in Canada
Crabtree Publishing
616 Welland Ave.
St. Catharines, Ontario L2M 5V6